Kids of Character

I Am Kind

By Juliet Concord

 **Gareth Stevens**
Publishing

Please visit our Web site, www.garethstevens.com. For a free color catalog of all our high-quality books, call toll free 1-800-542-2595 or fax 1-877-542-2596.

Library of Congress Cataloging-in-Publication Data

Concord, Juliet.
  I am kind / Juliet Concord.
     p. cm. — (Kids of character)
  Includes bibliographical references and index.
  ISBN 978-1-4339-4869-5 (pbk.)
  ISBN 978-1-4339-4870-1 (6-pack)
  ISBN 978-1-4339-4868-8 (library binding)
  1. Kindness–Juvenile literature. 2. Children–Conduct of life–Juvenile literature. I. Title.
  BJ1533.K5C66 2011
  177'.7–dc22
                                        2010036896

First Edition

Published in 2011 by
Gareth Stevens Publishing
111 East 14th Street, Suite 349
New York, NY 10003

Copyright © 2011 Gareth Stevens Publishing

Editor: Mary Ann Hoffman
Designer: Christopher Logan

Photo credits: Cover, pp. 5, 9, 17, 21 Shutterstock.com; p. 1 Jupiterimages/Pixland/Thinkstock; p. 7 Nick Daly/Photodisc/Thinkstock; p. 11 Hemera/Thinkstock; p. 13 George Doyle/Stockbyte/Thinkstock; pp. 15, 19 iStockphoto.com.

Printed in the United States of America

CPSIA compliance information: Batch #CW11GS: For further information contact Gareth Stevens, New York, New York at 1-800-542-2595.

Table of Contents

Boldface words appear in the glossary.

A Kind Person

A kind person helps others without being asked. A kind person is friendly and has good **manners**. A kind person thinks about how others feel. A kind person shares.

In the Neighborhood

Andy's neighbor was old. It was hard for her to **mow** the grass. Every week, Andy mowed his neighbor's lawn. Andy is kind.

Dee saw her friend fall off his bike. He was crying. Dee helped him get up. She rode home with him. Dee is kind.

At School

Carla's friend forgot to bring her snack to school. Carla had an apple. She gave it to her friend. Carla is kind.

A new girl got on the school bus. Jen asked the new girl to sit next to her. Jen talked to her. Jen walked into school with the new girl. Jen is kind.

Max is the fastest runner on the school team. Patty is not as fast as Max. Patty wants to be on the school team, too. Max goes running with Patty. Max is kind.

At Home

Ann's brother was having trouble with his homework. Ann helped him figure it out. Ann is kind.

Maria's sister Kim is saving for a new bike. Kim walks a neighbor's dog to earn money. One day, Kim was sick. Maria walked the dog for her. She gave Kim the money she earned. Maria is kind.

Ken's sister lost her doll. She looked sad. Ken gave her a hug. Ken is kind.

Glossary

manners: a polite way of acting

mow: to cut

For More Information

Books

Cuyler, Margery. *Kindness Is Cooler, Mrs. Ruler*. New York, NY: Simon & Schuster Books for Young Readers, 2007.

Snow, Todd, and Peggy Snow. *Kindness to Share from A to Z*. Oak Park Heights, MN: Maren Green Publishing, Inc., 2008.

Web Sites

Children's Kindness Network
www.ckn-usa.org
Watch a video and read about a kind cartoon cow.
Learn about ways to be kind.

Kindness Ideas
www.helpothers.org/ideas.php
Find ideas and links to show you how to be a kind person.

Index